~A BINGO BOOK~

Arkansas
Bingo Book

COMPLETE BINGO GAME IN A BOOK

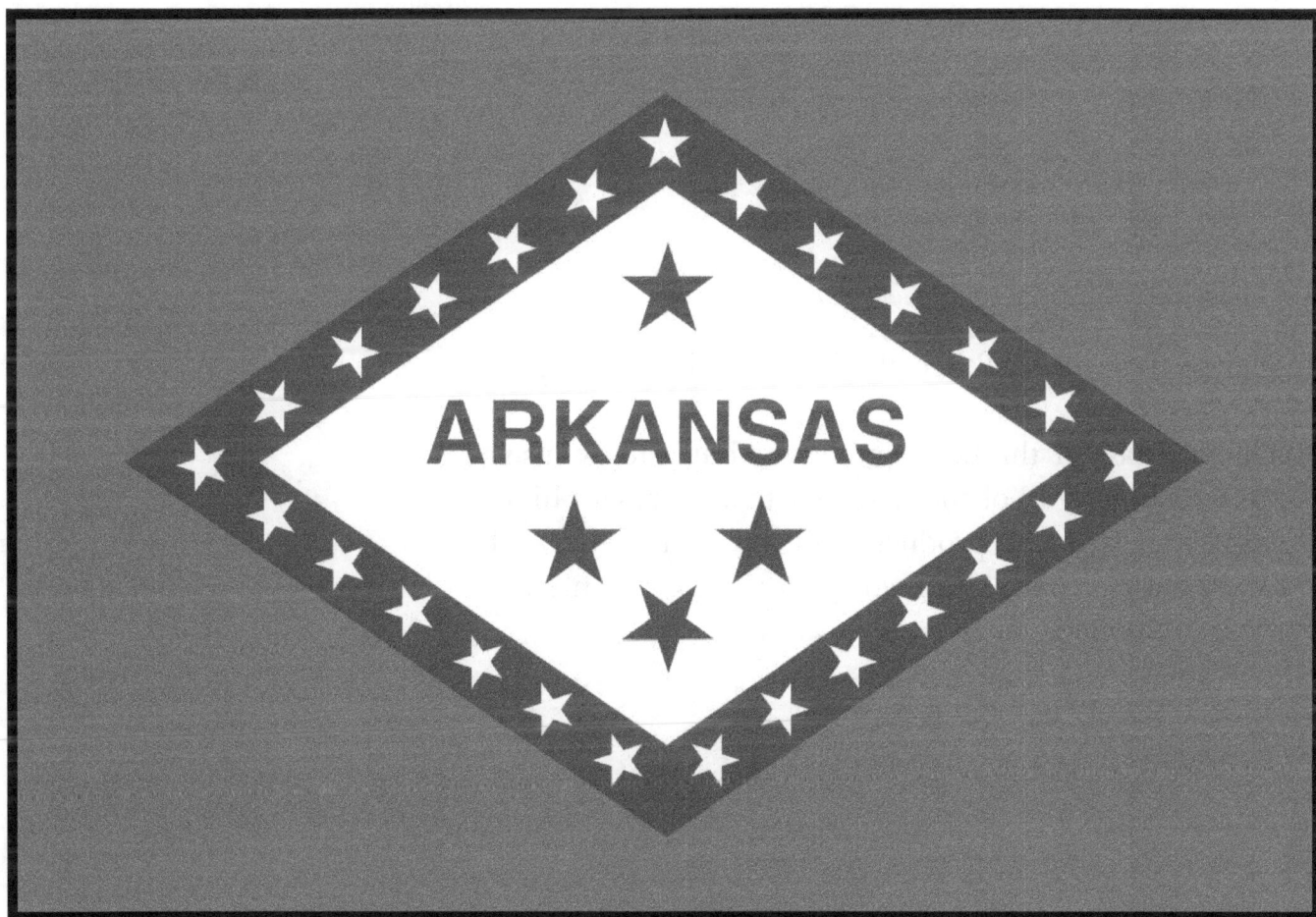

Written By Rebecca Stark

ISBN 978-0-87386-497-8

Educational Books 'n' Bingo

Printed in the U.S.A.

ARIZONA BINGO DIRECTIONS

INCLUDED:

List of Terms

Templates for Additional Terms and Clues

2 Clues per Term

30 Unique Bingo Cards

Markers

1. **Either cut apart the book or make copies of ALL the sheets. You might want to make an extra copy of the clue sheets to use for introduction and review. Keep the sheets in an envelope for easy reuse.**

2. Cut apart the call cards with terms and clues.

3. Pass out one bingo card per student. There are enough for a class of 30.

4. Pass out markers. You may cut apart the markers included in this book or use any other small items of your choice.

5. Decide whether or not you will require the entire card to be filled. Requiring the entire card to be filled provides a better review. However, if you have a short time to fill, you may prefer to have them do the just the border or some other format. Tell the class before you begin what is required.

6. There are 50 terms. Read the list before you begin. If there are any terms that have not been covered in class, you may want to read to the students the term and clues before you begin.

7. There is a blank space in the middle of each card. You can instruct the students to use it as a free space or you can write in answers to cover terms not included. Of course, in this case you would create your own clues. (Templates provided.)

8. Shuffle the cards and place them in a pile. Two or three clues are provided for each term. If you plan to play the game with the same group more than once, you might want to choose a different clue for each game. If not, you may choose to use more than one clue.

9. Be sure to keep the cards you have used for the present game in a separate pile. When a student calls, "Bingo," he or she will have to verify that the correct answers are on his or her card AND that the markers were placed in response to the proper questions. Pull out the cards that are on the student's card keeping them in the order they were used in the game. Read each clue as it was given and ask the student to identify the correct answer from his or her card.

10. If the student has the correct answers on the card AND has shown that they were marked in response to the *correct questions,* then that student is the winner and the game is over. If the student does not have the correct answers on the card OR he or she marked the answers in response to *the wrong questions,* then the game continues until there is a proper winner.

11. If you want to play again, reshuffle the cards and begin again.

Have fun!

TERMS

Arkansas Post

Arkansas River

Battle of Pea Ridge

Bentonville

Blanchard Springs Cavern

Border

Buffalo National River

Carpetbaggers

Climate

William Jefferson Clinton

Confederacy

Cotter

County (-ies)

Creed

Crowley's Ridge

Delta

Hernando de Soto

Diamond(s)

Diana Fritillary

Eureka Springs

Executive Branch

Fayetteville

Flag

Fort Smith

Highest Point

Honeybee

Hot Springs National Park

Jonesboro

Judicial Branch

Legislative Branch

Little Rock

Livestock

Louisiana Purchase

Mined

Mississippi River

Mockingbird

Motto

National Forests

Nickname

Ouachita(s)

Ozark

Pine

Plain

Quartz

Razorbacks

Rice

Song(s)

Tomato

University of Arkansas

White-tailed Deer

Additional Terms

Choose as many additional terms as you would like and write them in the squares. Repeat each as desired.
Cut out the squares and randomly distribute them to the class.
Instruct the students to place their square on the center space of their card.

Arkansas Bingo

Clues for Additional Terms

Write three clues for each of your additional terms.

_____	_____
1.	1.
2.	2.
3.	3.
_____	_____
1.	1.
2.	2.
3.	3.
_____	_____
1.	1.
2.	2.
3.	3.

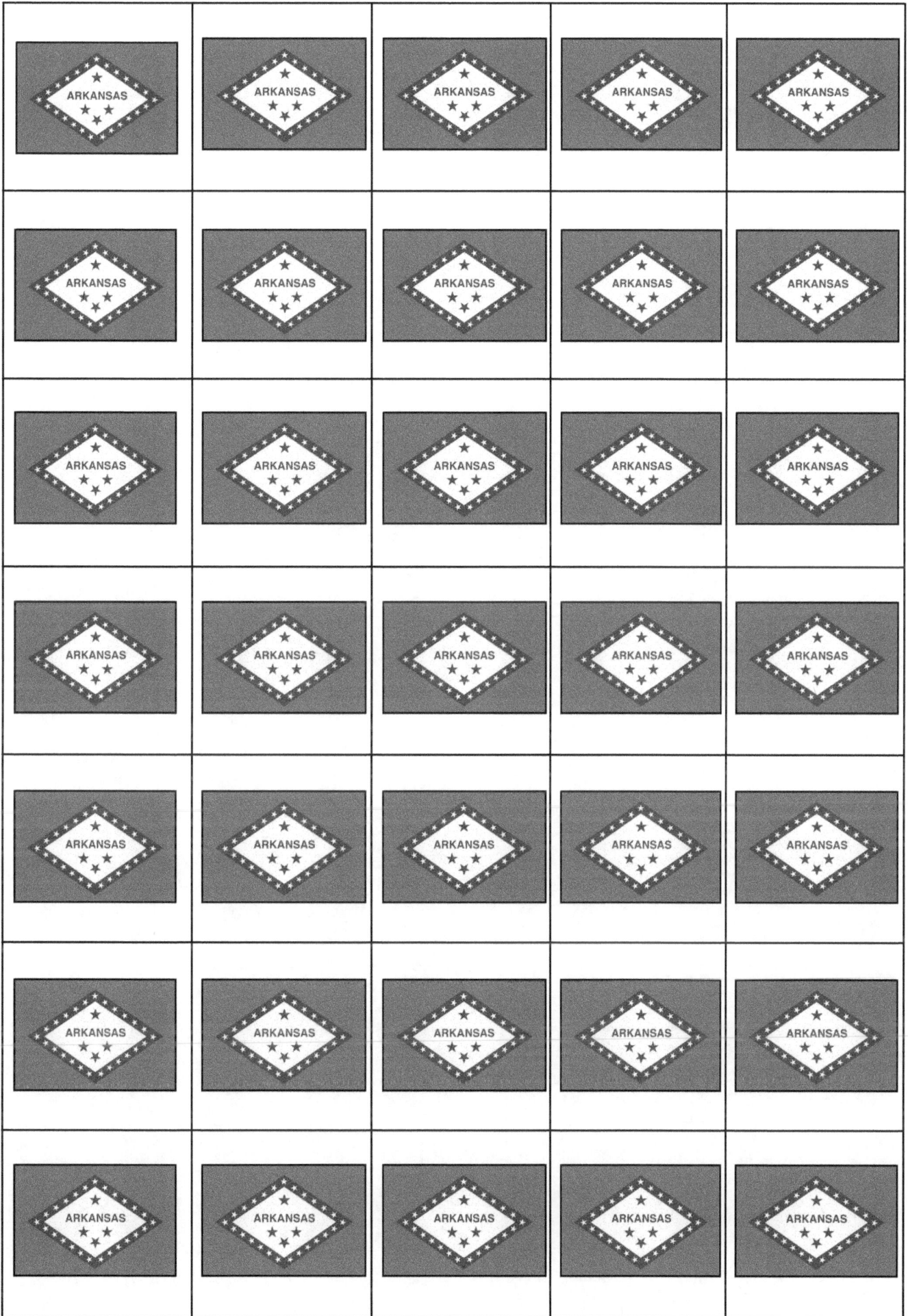

Arkansas Post 1. ___ was a French settlement at the site of a Quapaw Indian village. It was founded in 1686 as a trading post. 2. ___ was the capital of the Territory of Arkansas until Little Rock replaced it.	**Arkansas River** 1. The ___ is the largest river in the state. 2. The ___ Valley separates the Ozark Plateau to the north and the Ouachita Mountains to the south.
Battle of Pea Ridge 1. The ___ was a land battle of the American Civil War. It was fought from March 6 to March 8, 1862. 2. This Civil War battle gave the Union control of Missouri and led to the federal occupation of Arkansas.	**Bentonville** 1. Sam Walton's original Five and Dime is located in ___'s town square. 2. Crystal Bridges Museum of American Art is located in ___.
Blanchard Springs Cavern 1. This limestone cavern is located deep in the Ozark National Forest. 2. It is the only developed cave system operated by the U.S. Forest Service.	**Border** 1. These states ___ Arkansas: Missouri, Louisiana, Tennessee, Mississippi, Texas and Oklahoma. 2. The Mississippi River marks the eastern ___ of Arkansas.
Buffalo National River 1. The ___ was America's first national river. It is one of the few remaining undammed rivers in the lower 48 states. 2. The free-flowing ___ meanders through the heart of the Ozarks for 150 miles before joining the White River.	**Carpetbaggers** 1. ___ was the term Southerners gave to Northerners who moved to the South during the Reconstruction era. 2. The ___ was a negative term used during Reconstruction. It suggested exploitation by outsiders.
Climate 1. Arkansas has a temperate ___. Because of its central location, its ___ is affected by weather systems from all directions. 2. The state's ___ is warmer and more humid in the southern lowlands than in the mountainous regions.	**William Jefferson Clinton** 1. This President of the United States was born and raised in Arkansas. 2. Before he became the 42nd President of the United States, he was the governor of Arkansas.

Arkansas Bingo

Confederacy 1. Arkansas declared its secession from the Union on May 6, 1861, and joined the ___. 2. Arkansas joined the ___ in response to a call by President Lincoln for troops from each state to recapture Fort Sumter.	**Cotter** 1. This city is called "The Trout Capital of the U.S.A." 2. The clear cold waters of the White River attract fishermen from all over the world to ___ for trout fishing.
County (-ies) 1. There are 75 ___ in Arkansas. 2. Pulaski ___ is the largest one. Little Rock is the ___ seat.	**Creed** 1. A ___ is one or more basic beliefs that express values. 2. The first line of the Arkansas State ___ is "I believe in Arkansas as a land of opportunity and promise."
Crowley's Ridge 1. ___ is home to Jonesboro and other major cities of the Arkansas Delta. 2. ___ was formed when the Mississippi and Ohio rivers eroded away the land on each side; deposits of wind-blown soils added height to it.	**Delta** 1. The eastern part of Arkansas along the Mississippi Alluvial Plain is sometimes called the Arkansas ___. 2. Crowley's Ridge bisects the flat plain of the Arkansas ___.
Hernando de Soto 1. This Spanish explorer led an expedition into the southern United States. 2. ___ and his soldiers were the first Europeans to set foot in what is now Arkansas.	**Diamond(s)** 1. Crater of ___ State Park is the site of the only ___-producing mine in the United States. 2. The ___ is the state gem of Arkansas.
Diana Fritillary 1. The ___ is the state butterfly. 2. The wings of males of this species are dark brown with orange markings; females' wings are black with bright blue markings and white spots.	**Eureka Springs** 1. This city in Carroll County ___ is on the National Register of Historic Places. 2. Located in the Ozarks, the city has well preserved Victorian buildings.
Arkansas Bingo	© Barbara M. Peller

Executive Branch 1. The governor is head of the ___. The present-day governor is [fill in]. 2. The ___ includes the governor, lieutenant governor, attorney general, secretary of state, state treasurer, state auditor and the state land commissioner.	**Fayetteville** 1. ___ is the third largest city after Little Rock and Fort Smith. 2. The Arkansas Air and Military Museum is located in ___.
Flag 1. The stars below the state name on the ___ represent the 3 countries to which the territory belonged: France, Spain and the U.S.A. The single star above represents the Confederacy. 2. The 25 stars around the border of the diamond on the ___ represent Arkansas as the 25th state.	**Fort Smith** 1. This city on the Arkansas-Oklahoma border is the second largest city in Arkansas. 2. Isaac Charles Parker is known as the "Hanging Judge.'\" His courthouse in ___ is now a National Historic Site.
Highest Point 1. Magazine Mountain is the ___ point in Arkansas at 2,753 feet. 2. Complete this analogy: Magazine Mountain : ___ :: Ouachita River : lowest point	**Honeybee** 1. The ___ is the official state insect. 2. The ___ is the official state symbol in 17 states, probably because it plays such an important role in agriculture.
Hot Springs National Park 1. Many visitors go to ___ to experience the thermal waters. 2. Historic Fordyce Bathhouse is in ___.	**Jonesboro** 1. This city in Craighead County is the site of the main campus of Arkansas State University. 2. This college town in northeastern Arkansas is the fifth most populous city in Arkansas.
Judicial Branch 1. The ___ interprets what our laws mean and makes decisions about the laws and those who break them. 2. The ___ is made up of five court systems, the highest of which is the state Supreme Court. Arkansas Bingo	**Legislative Branch** 1. The ___ comprises the Arkansas Senate and the Arkansas House of Representatives. 2. The ___ makes the laws. © Barbara M. Peller

Little Rock 1. ___ is the capital and most populous city in the state. 2. The U.S. Arsenal Building is located in MacArthur Park in downtown ___. General Douglas MacArthur was born in this city.	**Livestock** 1. ___ products make up more than 60% of the state's agricultural revenue. 2. Broilers, or young chickens, account for more than 40% of the state's ___ production.
Louisiana Purchase 1. As a result of the ___, Arkansas became part of the District of Louisiana and the Territory of Orleans. 2. The ___ doubled the size of the United States.	**Mined** 1. Natural gas is the state's most important ___ product. Petroleum is the second most valuable. 2. Bromine and crushed stone are other important ___ products.
Mississippi River 1. The ___ forms most of the state's eastern border, separating it from Tennessee and Mississippi. 2. The Arkansas, White, and St. Francis rivers are all tributaries of the ___.	**Mockingbird** 1. The ___ is the official state bird of Arkansas. 2. This bird got its name because some species imitate the songs of other birds.
Motto 1. *"Regnat Populus"* is the state ___. It was originally adopted as an element of the state seal. 2. The state ___ translates from the Latin to "The People Rule."	**National Forests** 1. More than 2.9 million acres are included within the three ___ in Arkansas. 2. The Ozark National, the St. Francis, and the Ouachita are three ___.
Nickname 1. "The Natural State" is the ___ of Arkansas. 2. The ___ of Arkansas used to be "Land of Opportunity" and before that "The Wonder State." Arkansas Bingo	**Ouachita(s)** 1. The ___ Mountains are in west-central Arkansas. The highest peak in the state, is Mount Magazine, is in this range. 2. Unlike most other mountain ranges in the United States, the ___ run east and west rather than north and south. © Barbara M. Peller

Ozark

1. The ___ Plateau is sometimes referred to as the ___ Mountains. The region comprises three distinct uplifted, level plateaus.
2. The ___ Plateau comprises three plateaus: the Boston Plateau, or Mountains; the Springfield Plateau; and the Salem Plateau.

Pine

1. The ___ tree was chosen as the state tree because of its importance to the state's economy.
2. ___ timber resources are an important source of revenue for the state.

Plain

1. The Mississippi Alluvial ___ is a fertile area; it is sometimes referred to as the Delta Region.
2. The West Gulf Coastal ___ includes the southeastern and south-central portions of the state. This lowland area is characterized by pine forests and farmlands.

Quartz

1. ___ crystal is the official state mineral; bauxite is the state rock.
2. Mined in the Ouachita Mountains of Arkansas, ___ crystals are used in computers and sold to tourists.

Razorbacks

1. This is the nickname of athletic teams of University of Arkansas.
2. ___ are thin, long-legged wild hogs that are found in the state of Arkansas.

Rice

1. The most important crop in the state is ___. Soybeans, cotton, corn for grain, and wheat are also important.
2. Arkansas is the leading producer of this grain in the United States.

Song(s)

1. There are 4 official state ___: 2 state ___, 1 historical one, and 1 anthem.
2. The ___ that has been designated the official state anthem is "Arkansas," by Mrs. Eva Ware Barnett.

Tomato

1. The state fruit is the South Arkansas vine ripe pink ___.
2. The ___ is considered a fruit botanically, but is often used as a vegetable.

University of Arkansas

1. The main campus of the ___ is in Fayetteville.
2. The athletic teams of the ___ are nicknamed Razorbacks.

White-tailed Deer

1. The ___ is the state mammal.
2. The ___ is the state mammal of 11 states, including Arkansas. It is the most popular state mammal.

Arkansas Bingo

Arkansas Bingo

National Forests	Arkansas Post	Battle of Pea Ridge	Diana Fritillary	Blanchard Springs Cavern
Hernando de Soto	Arkansas River	Tomato	Legislative Branch	Ozark
Song(s)	Judicial Branch		Mississippi River	University of Arkansas
Rice	Ouachita(s)	Razorbacks	Jonesboro	Livestock
Mined	Fayetteville	Creed	Plain	Highest Point

Arkansas Bingo: Card No. 1

Arkansas Bingo

Rice	Song(s)	Fort Smith	Nickname	Hot Springs National Park
Livestock	Crowley's Ridge	Carpetbaggers	Ouachita(s)	Louisiana Purchase
William Jefferson Clinton	Fayetteville		Flag	Razorbacks
Mockingbird	Motto	Judicial Branch	White-tailed Deer	Blanchard Springs Cavern
Ozark	Tomato	Creed	Hernando de Soto	Plain

Arkansas Bingo: Card No. 2

Arkansas Bingo

Fayetteville	Razorbacks	Crowley's Ridge	Jonesboro	Song(s)
Livestock	Arkansas River	Climate	Arkansas Post	Executive Branch
Ouachita(s)	Tomato		Louisiana Purchase	Bentonville
Judicial Branch	William Jefferson Clinton	Mined	Mockingbird	Fort Smith
Plain	Confederacy	Creed	White-tailed Deer	Hot Springs National Park

Arkansas Bingo

Judicial Branch	Louisiana Purchase	Battle of Pea Ridge	Confederacy	Hot Springs National Park
Little Rock	Buffalo National River	Arkansas Post	Nickname	Song(s)
Mississippi River	Mockingbird		Highest Point	Diana Fritillary
Razorbacks	Arkansas River	Tomato	Creed	Carpetbaggers
Cotter	Ozark	Border	Plain	University of Arkansas

Arkansas Bingo

Ozark	Blanchard Springs Cavern	Ouachita(s)	Carpetbaggers	Confederacy
Little Rock	Razorbacks	Climate	Flag	Arkansas River
Battle of Pea Ridge	University of Arkansas		Legislative Branch	Eureka Springs
Highest Point	Hot Springs National Park	National Forests	White-tailed Deer	County (-ies)
Crowley's Ridge	Creed	Song(s)	Judicial Branch	Mississippi River

Arkansas Bingo

Bentonville	Louisiana Purchase	Fort Smith	Hot Springs National Park	University of Arkansas
Jonesboro	Ouachita(s)	County (-ies)	Arkansas Post	Song(s)
Nickname	Cotter		Buffalo National River	Flag
Creed	Mined	White-tailed Deer	Border	Battle of Pea Ridge
Livestock	Carpetbaggers	National Forests	Mississippi River	Delta

Arkansas Bingo

National Forests	Louisiana Purchase	Eureka Springs	Razorbacks	Crowley's Ridge
Livestock	Hot Springs National Park	Fayetteville	Arkansas River	Little Rock
University of Arkansas	Diana Fritillary		Flag	Buffalo National River
Judicial Branch	Mockingbird	Climate	Rice	William Jefferson Clinton
Creed	Confederacy	White-tailed Deer	Border	Bentonville

Arkansas Bingo

Mississippi River	Louisiana Purchase	Diamond(s)	Jonesboro	Buffalo National River
Little Rock	Battle of Pea Ridge	Nickname	University of Arkansas	Carpetbaggers
Delta	Confederacy		Hot Springs National Park	Blanchard Springs Cavern
Plain	Judicial Branch	Rice	Cotter	Mockingbird
Tomato	Creed	Border	Ouachita(s)	Livestock

Arkansas Bingo: Card No. 8

Arkansas Bingo

Flag	Crowley's Ridge	Fayetteville	Delta	Confederacy
Cotter	Hot Springs National Park	Mississippi River	Ouachita(s)	Louisiana Purchase
Executive Branch	National Forests		Arkansas River	Diamond(s)
County (-ies)	Blanchard Springs Cavern	Mined	Legislative Branch	Eureka Springs
Mockingbird	White-tailed Deer	Climate	Rice	Highest Point

Arkansas Bingo

Rice	Jonesboro	Buffalo National River	Nickname	Delta
University of Arkansas	Carpetbaggers	Arkansas Post	Arkansas River	Hot Springs National Park
Confederacy	Louisiana Purchase		Diana Fritillary	William Jefferson Clinton
Mined	Highest Point	County (-ies)	White-tailed Deer	Executive Branch
Climate	Livestock	Fort Smith	Ozark	Mississippi River

Arkansas Bingo

Bentonville	Louisiana Purchase	Ouachita(s)	County (-ies)	Livestock
Diamond(s)	Executive Branch	Legislative Branch	Flag	Arkansas Post
Little Rock	Hot Springs National Park		Fort Smith	Fayetteville
Climate	Song(s)	White-tailed Deer	Confederacy	Rice
Cotter	Creed	National Forests	Border	Crowley's Ridge

Arkansas Bingo

Crowley's Ridge	Blanchard Springs Cavern	Executive Branch	Jonesboro	Flag
Fayetteville	Livestock	Battle of Pea Ridge	Border	Arkansas River
National Forests	Eureka Springs		University of Arkansas	Nickname
Creed	Mockingbird	Hot Springs National Park	Rice	Little Rock
Louisiana Purchase	Diamond(s)	Confederacy	Cotter	Carpetbaggers

Arkansas Bingo

County (-ies)	Blanchard Springs Cavern	Bentonville	Executive Branch	University of Arkansas
Battle of Pea Ridge	Diamond(s)	Hot Springs National Park	Flag	William Jefferson Clinton
Jonesboro	Carpetbaggers		Fayetteville	Eureka Springs
Mississippi River	White-tailed Deer	Buffalo National River	Confederacy	Rice
Creed	Highest Point	Border	National Forests	Legislative Branch

Arkansas Bingo

Hernando de Soto	Hot Springs National Park	Ouachita(s)	Flag	Cotter
Carpetbaggers	National Forests	Executive Branch	Arkansas River	Louisiana Purchase
County (-ies)	Diana Fritillary		Fort Smith	Climate
Highest Point	White-tailed Deer	Confederacy	Buffalo National River	Bentonville
Creed	Nickname	William Jefferson Clinton	Livestock	Mississippi River

Arkansas Bingo: Card No. 14

Arkansas Bingo

Legislative Branch	Flag	Ouachita(s)	Crowley's Ridge	Jonesboro
Bentonville	Fort Smith	Arkansas Post	Battle of Pea Ridge	Cotter
University of Arkansas	National Forests		Song(s)	Louisiana Purchase
Creed	Executive Branch	Diamond(s)	White-tailed Deer	County (-ies)
Livestock	Mockingbird	Border	Delta	Fayetteville

Arkansas Bingo

Buffalo National River	Executive Branch	Diamond(s)	Delta	Motto
Nickname	William Jefferson Clinton	Eureka Springs	Little Rock	Diana Fritillary
County (-ies)	Blanchard Springs Cavern		University of Arkansas	Fayetteville
Judicial Branch	Carpetbaggers	Creed	Legislative Branch	Rice
Cotter	Quartz	Border	Mockingbird	Louisiana Purchase

Arkansas Bingo: Card No. 16

Arkansas Bingo

Climate	Pine	Honeybee	Executive Branch	Hernando de Soto
Legislative Branch	Cotter	White-tailed Deer	Diana Fritillary	Eureka Springs
Flag	Mississippi River		Quartz	Diamond(s)
Highest Point	Livestock	Rice	Ouachita(s)	William Jefferson Clinton
Mined	County (-ies)	Crowley's Ridge	Jonesboro	Blanchard Springs Cavern

Arkansas Bingo

Delta	Confederacy	Carpetbaggers	County (-ies)	Nickname
Louisiana Purchase	Climate	Mined	University of Arkansas	Cotter
Flag	William Jefferson Clinton		Honeybee	Battle of Pea Ridge
Blanchard Springs Cavern	Arkansas Post	White-tailed Deer	Rice	Fort Smith
Quartz	Executive Branch	Ouachita(s)	Pine	Bentonville

Arkansas Bingo

University of Arkansas	Bentonville	Executive Branch	Diamond(s)	Rice
Legislative Branch	Jonesboro	Louisiana Purchase	Crowley's Ridge	Diana Fritillary
Pine	Confederacy		Arkansas River	Song(s)
Fort Smith	Quartz	Mined	Mockingbird	Honeybee
Battle of Pea Ridge	Motto	Livestock	Mississippi River	Border

Arkansas Bingo

Hernando de Soto	Pine	Jonesboro	Executive Branch	Border
Carpetbaggers	Fayetteville	Little Rock	Mined	Nickname
Blanchard Springs Cavern	Eureka Springs		Judicial Branch	Arkansas Post
Ozark	Tomato	Plain	Mockingbird	Quartz
Razorbacks	Mississippi River	Motto	Rice	Honeybee

Arkansas Bingo: Card No. 20

Arkansas Bingo

Legislative Branch	Bentonville	Little Rock	Executive Branch	Ozark
Blanchard Springs Cavern	Honeybee	Buffalo National River	Diamond(s)	National Forests
William Jefferson Clinton	Livestock		Pine	Ouachita(s)
Mined	Crowley's Ridge	Quartz	Highest Point	Mississippi River
Judicial Branch	Motto	Border	Climate	Mockingbird

Arkansas Bingo

Delta	Fort Smith	Honeybee	Battle of Pea Ridge	County (-ies)
Nickname	Jonesboro	Song(s)	Diamond(s)	Arkansas River
Carpetbaggers	Diana Fritillary		National Forests	Eureka Springs
Quartz	Highest Point	Mockingbird	Arkansas Post	Little Rock
Motto	Climate	Pine	William Jefferson Clinton	Mississippi River

Arkansas Bingo

Buffalo National River	Pine	Crowley's Ridge	Battle of Pea Ridge	Border
Bentonville	Hernando de Soto	Livestock	Legislative Branch	Arkansas Post
Fort Smith	County (-ies)		Plain	National Forests
William Jefferson Clinton	Motto	Quartz	Climate	Mockingbird
Ozark	Tomato	Mississippi River	Mined	Honeybee

Arkansas Bingo

Buffalo National River	Mississippi River	Hernando de Soto	Pine	Diamond(s)
Honeybee	Border	Little Rock	Nickname	National Forests
Eureka Springs	Delta		County (-ies)	William Jefferson Clinton
Ozark	Plain	Quartz	Climate	Blanchard Springs Cavern
Razorbacks	Judicial Branch	Motto	Jonesboro	Tomato

Arkansas Bingo

Judicial Branch	Little Rock	Pine	Ouachita(s)	Honeybee
Arkansas Post	Blanchard Springs Cavern	Legislative Branch	Buffalo National River	Arkansas River
Highest Point	Diamond(s)		Plain	Quartz
Song(s)	Ozark	Tomato	Motto	Diana Fritillary
Border	Hernando de Soto	Carpetbaggers	Cotter	Razorbacks

Arkansas Bingo

Honeybee	Pine	Fort Smith	Nickname	Delta
Mined	Jonesboro	Diamond(s)	Hernando de Soto	Buffalo National River
Highest Point	Plain		Diana Fritillary	Judicial Branch
Climate	Battle of Pea Ridge	Ozark	Motto	Quartz
Eureka Springs	Cotter	Ouachita(s)	Tomato	Razorbacks

Arkansas Bingo

Fort Smith	Carpetbaggers	Pine	Hernando de Soto	Fayetteville
Ozark	Plain	Legislative Branch	Quartz	Arkansas River
White-tailed Deer	Tomato		Motto	Judicial Branch
Delta	Bentonville	Little Rock	Razorbacks	Arkansas Post
Cotter	Diana Fritillary	Honeybee	Song(s)	Eureka Springs

Arkansas Bingo: Card No. 27

Arkansas Bingo

Fort Smith	Hernando de Soto	Song(s)	Pine	Buffalo National River
Fayetteville	Honeybee	Plain	Nickname	Diana Fritillary
Tomato	William Jefferson Clinton		Eureka Springs	Mined
Rice	Delta	Livestock	Motto	Quartz
Battle of Pea Ridge	Flag	Cotter	Razorbacks	Ozark

Arkansas Bingo

Honeybee	Hernando de Soto	Delta	Legislative Branch	Flag
Mockingbird	Mined	Little Rock	Eureka Springs	Song(s)
Highest Point	Plain		Arkansas River	Pine
Fayetteville	Ozark	Hot Springs National Park	Motto	Quartz
Buffalo National River	Diamond(s)	Razorbacks	Bentonville	Tomato

Arkansas Bingo: Card No. 29

Arkansas Bingo

Confederacy	Pine	Nickname	Flag	Quartz
Arkansas Post	Hernando de Soto	Fort Smith	Diana Fritillary	Arkansas River
Highest Point	County (-ies)		Eureka Springs	Little Rock
Razorbacks	Bentonville	Battle of Pea Ridge	Motto	Plain
Ozark	University of Arkansas	Tomato	Honeybee	Song(s)

© Barbara M. Peller

www.ingramcontent.com/pod-product-compliance
Lightning Source LLC
LaVergne TN
LVHW061337060426
835511LV00014B/1963